For Sandra

How To Make Money Today

Contents

Introduction	3
All Roads Are Not Paved With Gold	3
Friends And Family Thought I Was Mad	4
Entry To Market	5
How To Make Money Idea Number 1	7
How To Make Money Idea Number 2	12
How To Make Money Idea Number 3	18
How To Make Money Idea Number 4	19
How To Make Money Idea Number 5	20
How To Make Money Idea Number 6	23
How To Make Money Idea Number 7	24
Conclusions	25

Introduction

Most people earn money via a job where you give your skills and time for a salary. There is nothing wrong with this I was a freelance I.T. consultant for over 25 years and was paid handsomely for my skills and time. But there is one problem, if you are not commission based such as in sales or on large bonuses as a result of trading stock markets then it does not scale. In other words you will hit a salary cap unless you can clone yourself which I very much doubt. You could do more than one job but the principal is the same. I will be brutally honest here if you trade your time for money you are taking the easy path in life! I heard a great quote "Taking easy decision results in a hard life". The best approach would be to do a job and take a salary whilst building other income streams. Once the money from these streams is greater than your current salary quit your salaried job. But guess what this is what really happens, you get a job, you get in from work, put your feet up, watch TV etc. You do not invest time in investigating other income streams so you are trapped in this cycle. What compounds this is that you increase your lifestyle costs when you get a salary increase or a better job. You buy a better car or a bigger house as we need to keep up with the Joneses! Does this sound familiar? I bet it does I have been there trust me.

I was a consumer and not a producer back in the old days, nice cars and holidays then one day I had a wakeup call that came out of the blue. This is how I woke up I had got to a point where I was earning between £15K to £20k per month before tax and expenses. I had increased this income over the years by learning new skills working longer hours plus working overtime and weekend work. I suddenly realised I had hit an income ceiling plus working long hours constantly was like holding a tiger by the tail.

So what did I do next?

All Roads Are Not Paved With Gold

When I started on my journey I watched the endless videos on how to make money and believe me there are some wild claims out there in fact crazy ones at that. They normally were followed by a link to the course they were selling I think we know how they were making their money. Believe me there is no easy way to make money it requires dedication and understanding of all aspects of business. You need to let all emotions disappear during your journey and be prepared for many setbacks. Make sure you understand your business ideas and do your due diligence before jumping in head first.

You also need to be prepared for a very long journey, forget weekend recreation its 7 days per week to get your business ideas started. One other thing you must be prepared to do is to scrap your business idea if you hit showstoppers or you have misunderstood the market. This happened to me more than once. I entered the Yoga and bags retail businesses and could not afford the Google search costs per click so there was no website traffic and thus no sales, more on this later.

One final comment stay away from all the bullshit videos out there claiming you will make thousands of pounds per day, it is all rubbish.

Friends and Family Thought I Was Mad

I would hear the words **"You are giving up that income per month? I wish I earned it."** would be the order of the day. To be honest and you might think I was being selfish the money was good but it became sole destroying after a while. I was trading a great deal of my time for it plus in addition losing time with my family which I could not get back. I was also becoming frustrated as the income scaling problem was constantly nagging me. I would be constantly asking myself two important questions,

1. How do I scale and make more money efficiently.
2. How do I make this money passively 24x7 on autopilot.

This really halted my momentum and I lost interest with the salaried life even though I was freelance. I knew if I carried on doing this for another 10 years nothing would change and this really shook me up.

In the end I used to dread Sundays especially in the afternoon as I would know I would be away all week in Germany or Belgium etc. It was on Monday a sunny morning about 7am and I decided enough was enough I was at Manchester Airport I had already checked in for my flight and I was watching foxes playing in a documentary being screened on the airport television. I went to the flight desk and asked for my bags to be taken off the aircraft and I jumped into a taxi and went home. I must confess it was the best decision I have ever made I felt a huge weight had been lifted off my shoulders.

I thought a fresh new start outside the I.T. freelance world would be easy and a dream come true how wrong I was it was sheer hell!

The business world verses salaried employment these are worlds apart and there is no comparison. I must confess now I appreciate how company owners who pay employees salaries should be applauded that does not include companies using slave labour or sweat shops of course.

Once I had a couple of weeks to get my head around how I would make money I formed a plan. I had approximately £70K in savings so I could cover the bills quite easily for a year. One thing I must say £70K disappears very quickly!

Entry To Market

This is probably one chapter in this book you need to remember and I wish someone had told me this earlier on in my journey. You might think what I am going to explain is obvious but it is not as your emotions and enthusiasm can get the better of you when looking into new money making ideas. When you look at ideas to make money ask yourself this one question?

"How easy is it to enter the market?"

In other words how many other people are on this road and is the road busy? If the road is busy leave this money making idea alone. Ideally you are looking for a road that is not congested and these roads present the best opportunities as they are easier to enter. These roads do require hard work and most people do not like these types of road.

I will give you a great example of this and these are my opinions everyone has heard of **eBay** it has been around for many years and the number of worldwide sellers on **eBay** grows by the day. I want to take you through a scenario which will enforce what I have just stated. I want to use pet products niche on eBay and use for example a **dog collar** product. There are so many people selling dog collars ask yourself how do you compete?

Ideas on how to compete in busy markets.

1. Better dog collar than your competition.
2. Cheaper retail price.
3. The product adds value.

The screenshot below shows an eBay product search in the Pet Supplies category for our search term **dog collars**. I have underlined in blue how many results there were for this search term and it was 160,000. In other words there are 160,000 **dog collar** products listed for sale. Now you could argue I am using a broad search keyword phrase search term and yes I am so let us refine our search and target **blue dog collars**.

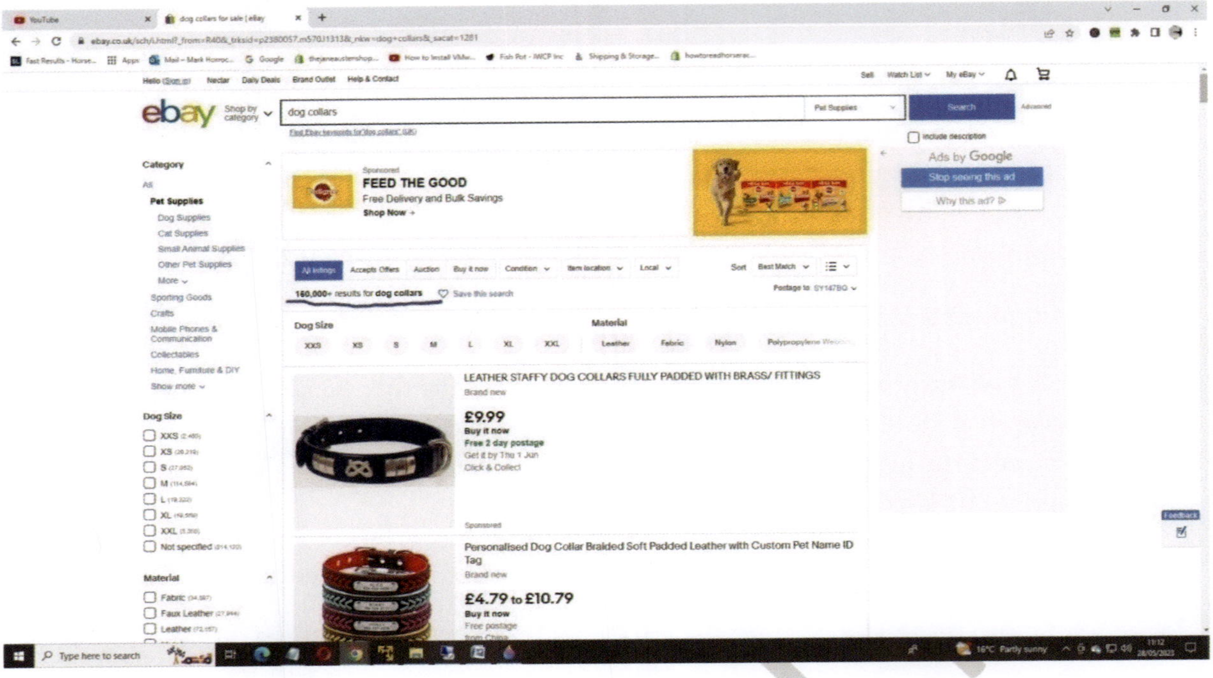

In the screenshot below our search for **blue dog collars** returns 57,000 product listings. This is still too many listings and thus too much competition.

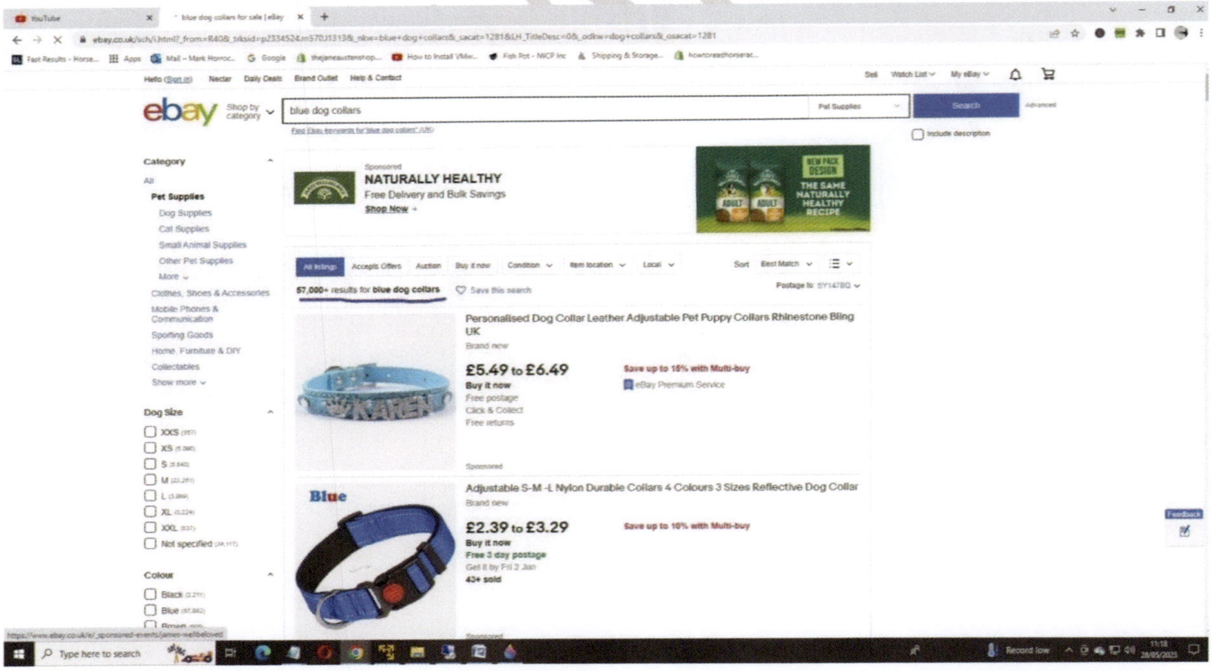

Remember if your product is not on the top 3 pages of eBay you will struggle selling your products or services.

Now let us look at the sporting goods category on eBay and our search term is **vintage hardy reels**. If you look at the screenshot below our search has returned 567 product listings so there is less competition. Now this is a specialised niche so you would probably be able to get sales in this niche but would it scale probably not.

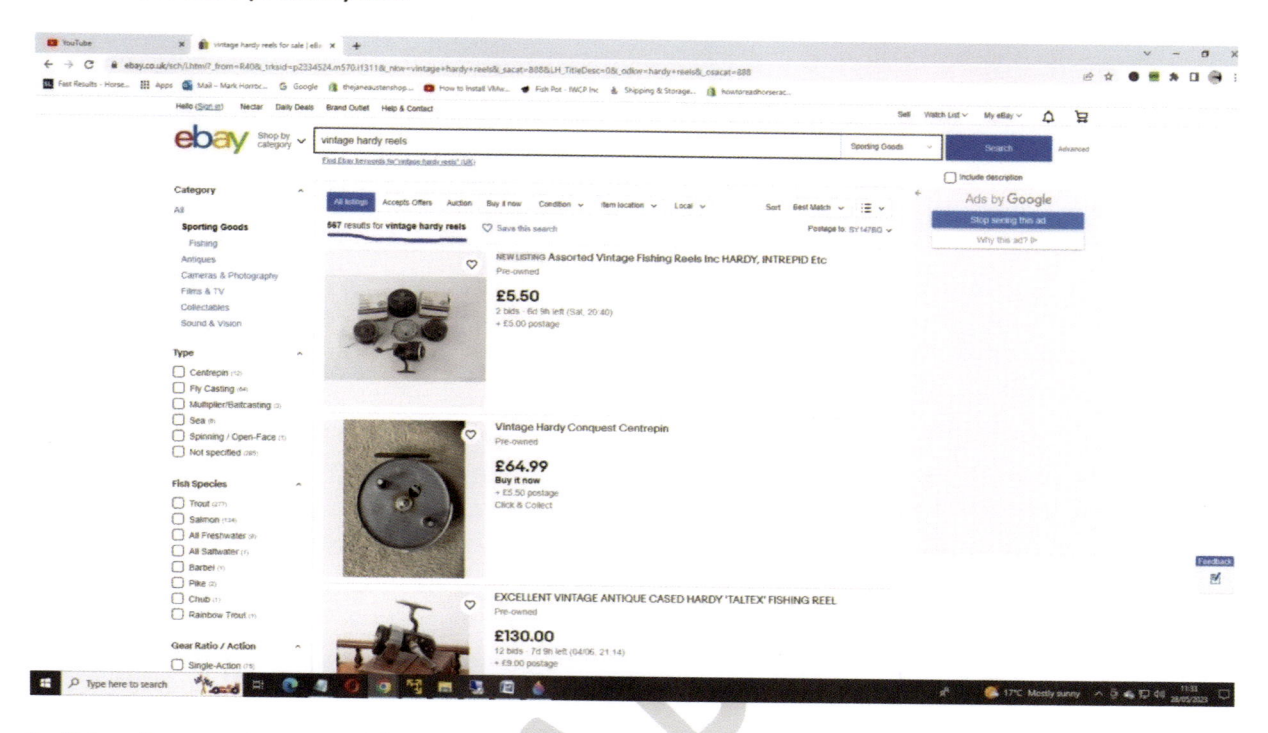

I will touch on my journey with eBay as a way to make money in another chapter.

How To Make Money Idea Number 1.

Affiliate Marketing

Now you will say I know about this already but just wait a minute and read on please. I fell into the affiliate marketing area by watching too many YouTube videos! I thought how easy this would be, how wrong I was and I will explain the various affiliate making money ideas I actually tried.

Clickbank

https://www.clickbank.com/

This is a platform that allows you to promote other peoples products in return for an affiliate income and sometimes a recurring income. Now **Clickbank** has been around for many years and is very popular. You can promote different categories of products like beauty, weight loss and yoga and many more via Clickbank. It is relatively easy to use - you just get a link to the product you are promoting and you are under starter's orders making money passively, wrong!

So where do we promote our Clickbank affiliate product links to get potential customers and revenue?

First approach is to write a blog or create a website these are relatively easy to do but now you hit another problem how do you get traffic to your blog or website. New blogs or websites will not rank organically immediately in the Google search engine. You can be waiting months or years to rank organically on page one of Google. It also involves you writing natural content that highlights your promoted Clickbank products to appear on page one of Google.

So how do you get immediate traffic and results?

You can pin your Clickbank product link on other people's established blog posts which focus on your niche. Another way is to use social media sites like Pinterest or Facebook and Instagram. You can also setup a YouTube channel and put your product links in your videos but you have to get video views for it to be effective. I actually took a different route I used Google Adwords PPC – Pay Per Click. In other words I paid for traffic to my blog or website. You basically choose your keywords or search terms that are appropriate to your products and the keywords or search terms that will be used by potential customers searching for your products.

I used Google Adwords for PPC – Pay Per Click. I must confess I had a steep learning curve here in how to configure it and it is something that you have to understand well before diving into it. I made so many mistakes here and it cost me financially.

Please see screenshot of Google Adwords website dashboard.

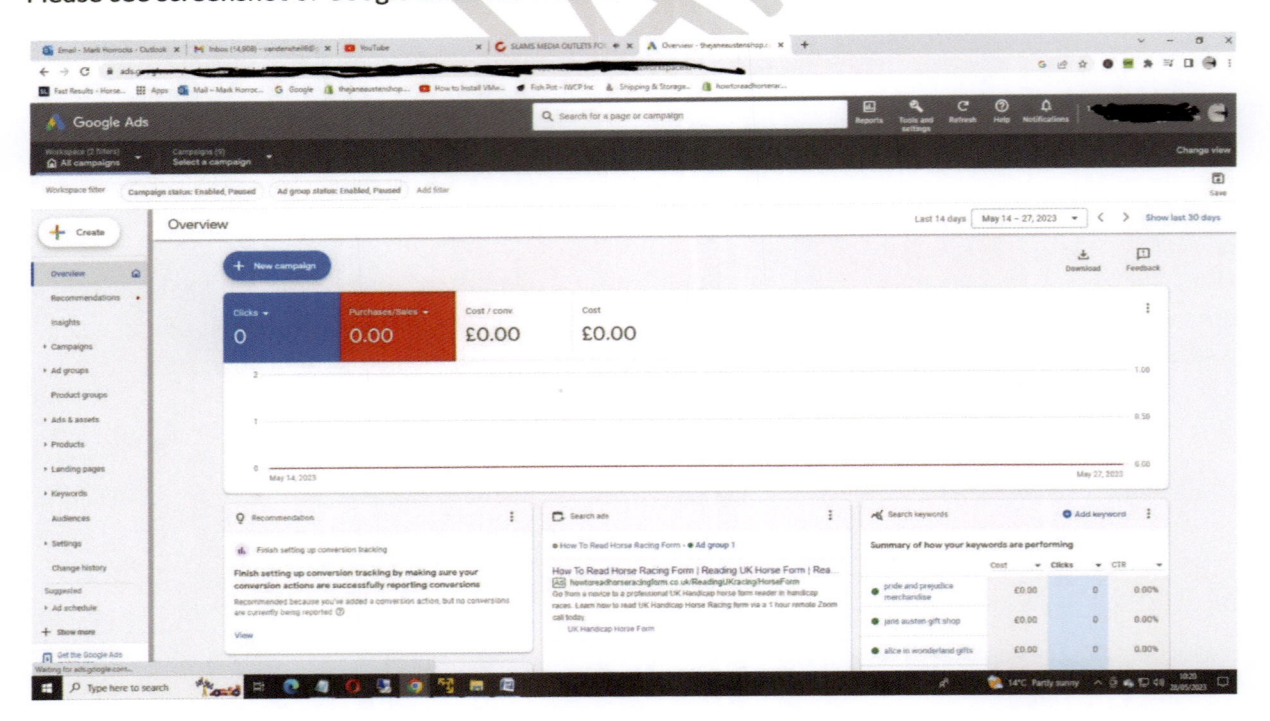

You can see from the screenshot below showing my Clickbank account and sales. If you look at the sales for Mon May22 pointed to by the blue line you see I earned $7.42. Now I have not used

Clickbank for many years but I still make money passively from it as my affiliate product links still exist on social media websites such as Pinterest etc.

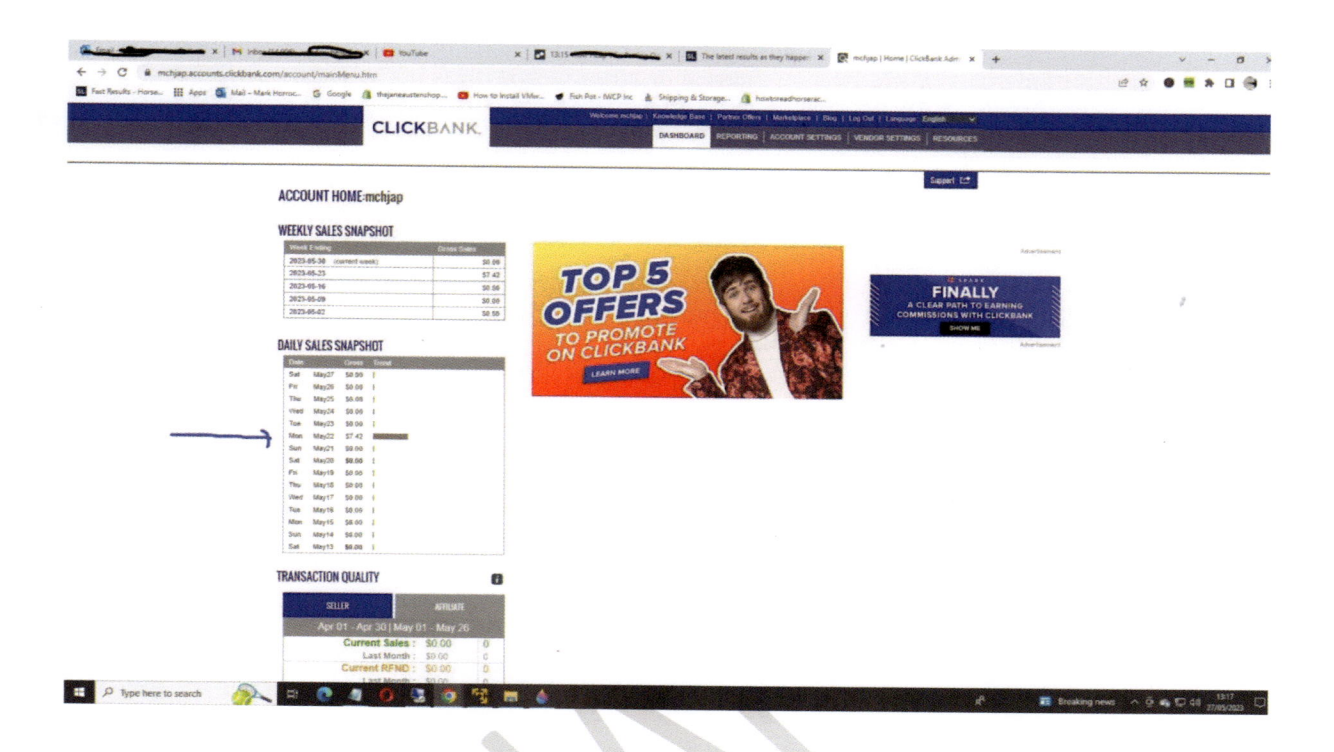

In the screenshot below you can see another Clickbank market place in the Health & Fitness niche.

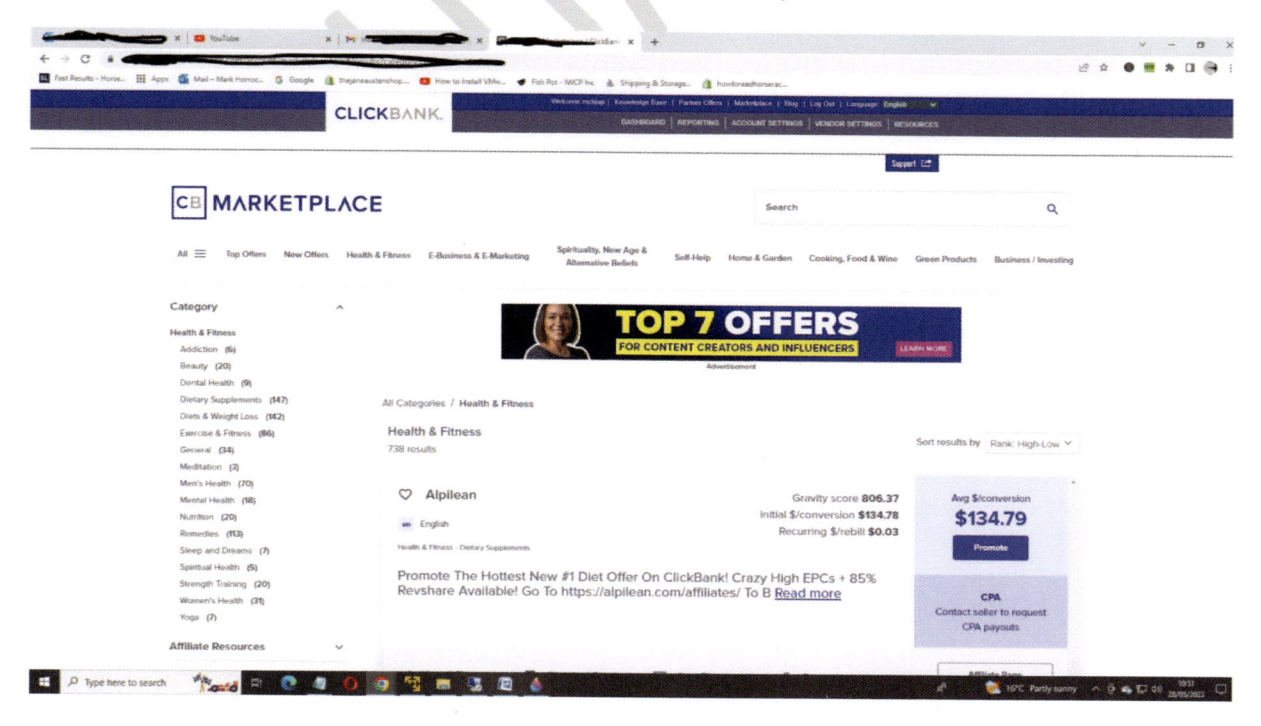

You see the product **Alpilean** in the screenshot above you can make **$134.79** affiliate commission if you sell this product.

You can make money with Clickbank and I have, but the problem I encountered was the financial cost of driving traffic to my websites and blogs to promote these affiliate products via PPC – Pay Per Click. PPC was eating up all of my affiliate income in other words I was making little profit after operating costs. When you use PPC you should view it for example as spending one pound to make 5 pounds profit afters operating costs etc. I was actually losing money with this strategy as the market place was easy to enter and there was lots of competition. This made the PPC expensive due to the market saturation. Please see Google search screenshot below for **dog collars**. There are 29,800,000 search results for **dog collars**.

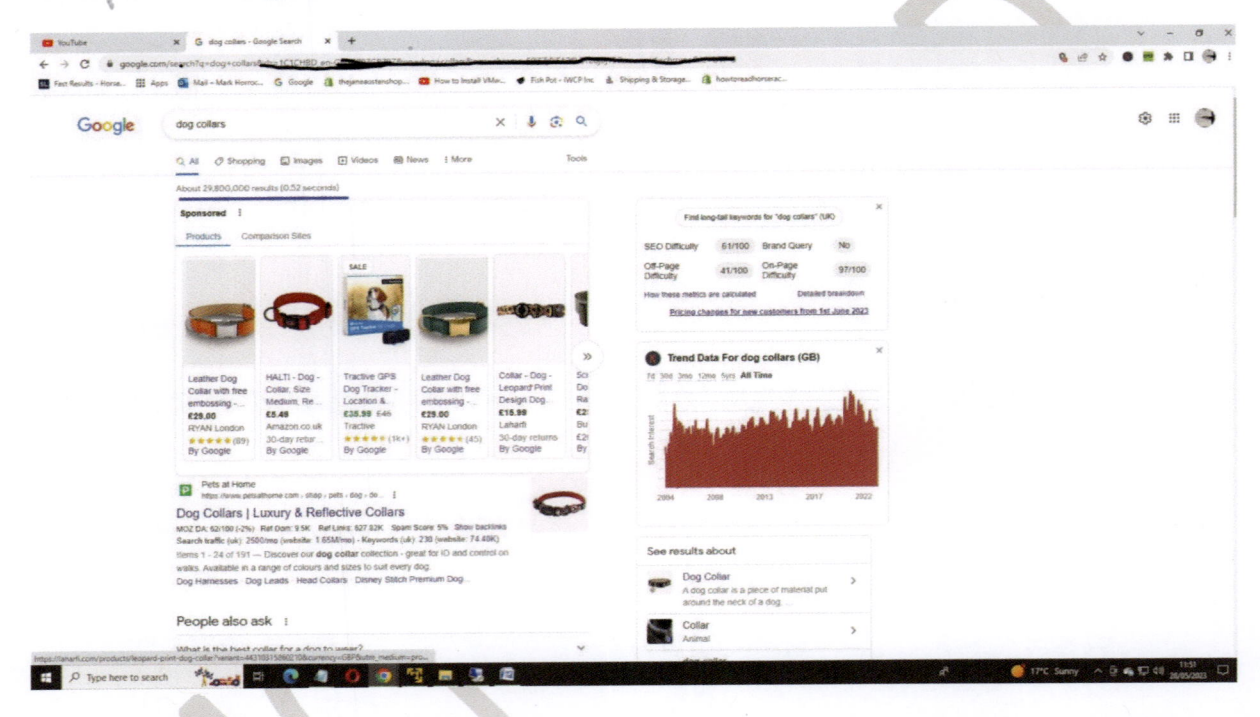

If your product does not appear on the top 3 pages of Google you will have a hard time selling dog collars.

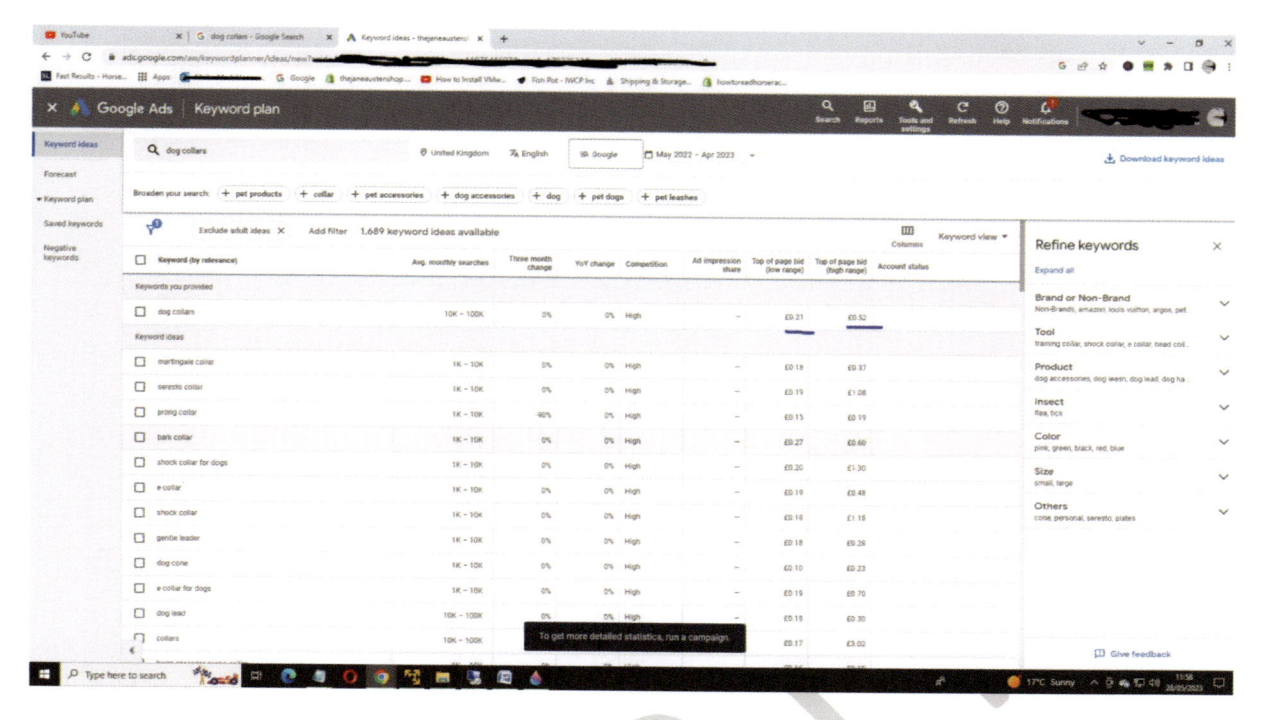

If you look at the above screenshot it shows the Google Adwords PPC for keyword phrases around **dog collars** for UK only. You can see underlined in blue the low and high cost for dog collars is between £0.21 and £0.52 per click. If we look at this further and let's say we had 100 clicks per day at £0.50 per click this would equate to a PPC cost spend of £50 per day that is approximately £1500 per month.

The best approach is to play the long game and place your affiliate product links on free social media sites like Pinterest which costs nothing. Some affiliate marketers make a great amount of money from Clickbank I found it was not for me. Clickbank and eBay are saturated markets in my opinion and they also fail one key component of making money and that is you do not have control. I will give you an example of this. Let us say we have our eBay store and we are selling products or services we then start to get negative customer feedback which might be your fault or not your eBay ratings will be reduced which affects sales. You can also get suspended if you do other misdemeanours on eBay I know it happened to me a number of times with the suspension duration getting lengthier each time this happened.

Amazon and eBay Affiliate

Affiliate marketing is promoting products that are currently being sold on Amazon or eBay this is straight forward you open accounts on each platform as an affiliate marketer and you are now up and running. How wrong, you still have the same problems as with Clickbank where do you place your affiliate product links and how do you get traffic to these affiliate product links. You will hit the same problems I mentioned using Clickbank affiliate marketing the main one being cost of acquiring website or blog traffic. There is an even bigger problem with this type of affiliate marketing is that the percentage revenue received from each sale of a products is small. Your PPC – Pay Per Click costs will wipe out any profits very quickly I have been down this route and it proved to be bad business.

Once again you should post your affiliate product links on free social media sites such as Pinterest and Instagram and play the long game.

The biggest problems I see with affiliate marketing is that it has been around for many years and it is an easy road to enter in other words anyone can do it. I tried this for about a year but found the traffic costs and the irregularity of receiving revenue was a problem. I now just take small revenue from old affiliate links posted on social media many years ago.

How To Make Money Idea Number 2

Drop Shipping

https://www.aliexpress.com/

https://www.fiverr.com/

https://www.shopify.com/

I have spent over 6 years using the well known drop shipping method where you list other people's products and sell these at a higher retail value thus making a profit. The amount of profit you want to make is up to you. The main drop shipping site I use is **AliExpress.com** based in China but there are many other sites you can use. The only downside to AliExpress.com is that the shipping times are quite lengthy between 2 and 4 weeks. Normally a product purchased on AliExpress.com would be shipped directly to the customer but I like the products shipped to me first and then I would forward on to the customer. This made tracking easier and also you can re-package your purchased products as your own brand. The profit margin was 3 to 4 times the product cost price so it was still very lucrative.

So how do you promote your products?

My approach was to use a very good ecommerce platform called Shopify which makes creating retail websites very easy. It handles all customer checkouts and payments and makes it very easy and secure for customers purchasing your products. Please see Shopify screenshot below,

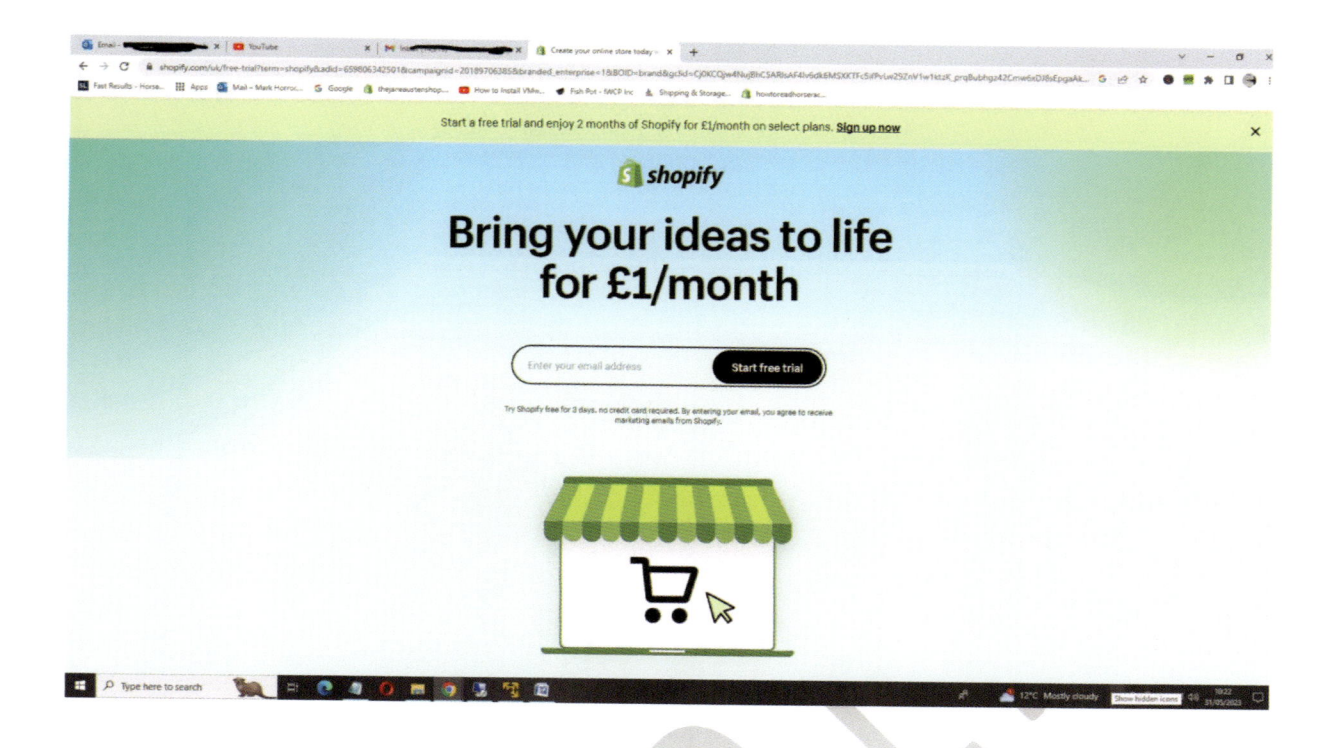

For my website logo and favicon design I always use the great outsourcing site Fiverr.com see screenshot below. It's not that expensive and I have been using it for many years. I personally built my own website using Shopify as I have a strong technical background.

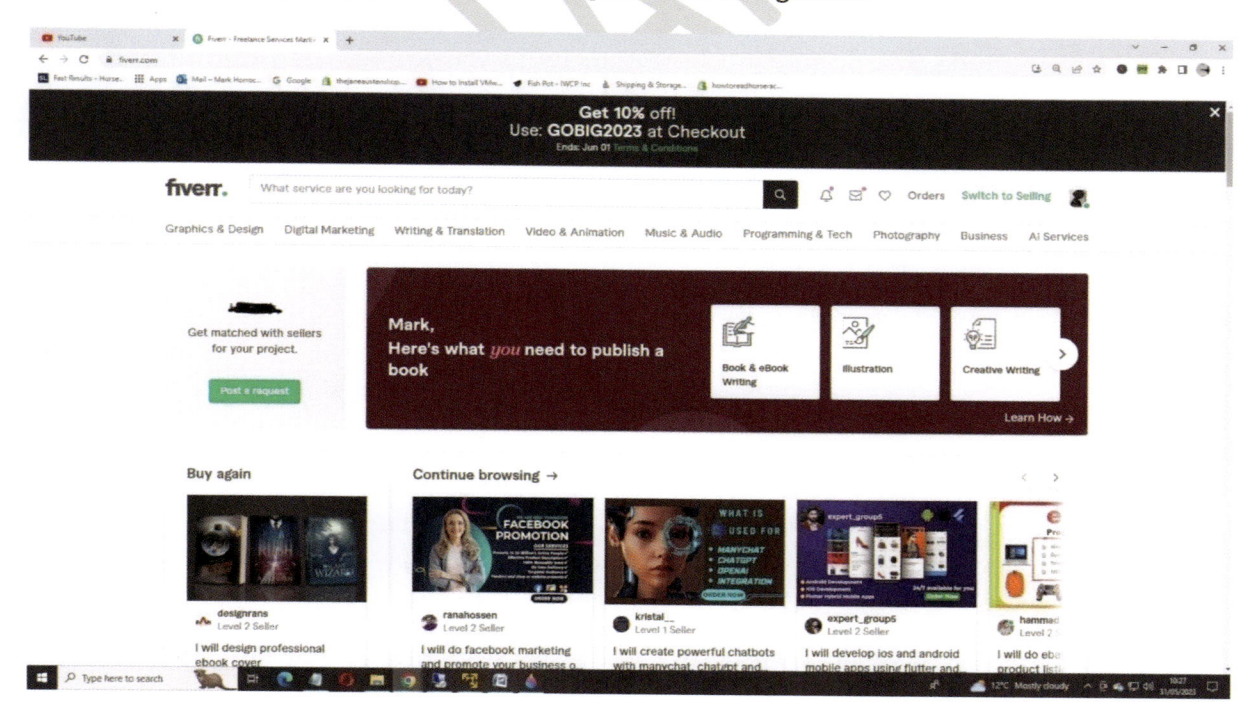

It would take me approximately 3 days to implement a new retail website using Shopify that includes all product listings or services plus website images, logo and favicon plus content. We need to have quality traffic to our website in order to get sales. I tried the 5 approaches below some using paid traffic and some with free traffic.

1. Google Adwords
2. Facebook
3. Bing
4. Pinterest
5. Organic Traffic

Google Adwords

https://ads.google.com/

We touched on this earlier and this is by far the best way to achieve quality traffic to your retail website. I had to learn the structure of Google Adwords with respect to the configuration of keywords, campaigns and adverts. I did not want to pay somebody to implement this for me I wanted to be in control. At the start I wasted so much money on the PPC – Pay Per Click due to my badly configured Adwords campaigns and it cost me financially. Over a period of time I learnt by my mistakes and I am now very competent in this area. Some key things to remember when setting up your Adwords campaigns which I wish I would have known in advance.

1. Understand what search terms in Google customers are using to find your products this is very important. Use the Adwords keyword tool I mentioned earlier in the book to see what the cost per click – PPC is for the search terms. Try using long tail keywords these are search terms that contain 2 or more words,

   e.g.

   Blue leather dog collar

2. Your keywords must be relevant to your website landing/product pages and adverts. Adwords measure this by a quality score being assigned to each keyword. A quality score of 10 is the best and this can result in cheaper potential customer clicks on your adverts.

3. It also important to understand which countries your customers are located in, there is no point spending money targeting countries which will not purchase your products.

4. What gender and age is your target audience and what time of the day do you expect to get sales or conversions these are important questions.

There is a great deal to learn with Adwords and in this book it is not my intention to explain this in detail.

One key Google tool that works with Adwords is Google Analytics were you can analyse what search terms customers are using and which keywords are getting sales (conversions). This allows you to spend your PPC budget on keywords that are converting to sales.

You basically link your Google analytics to your Google Adwords account and the data is collected automatically 24x7.

See screenshot below. You can see the Google Analytics screen displaying useful data such as sessions by country and users by time of day. Plus you can see how you acquire users e.g. Organic search etc.

There is so much data to drill down on to improve sales and reduce cost per click for your Adwords advertising campaigns.

You need to understand your customers and target them effectively constantly refining the keywords in your PPC eliminating keywords or search terms that do not generate sales or conversions.

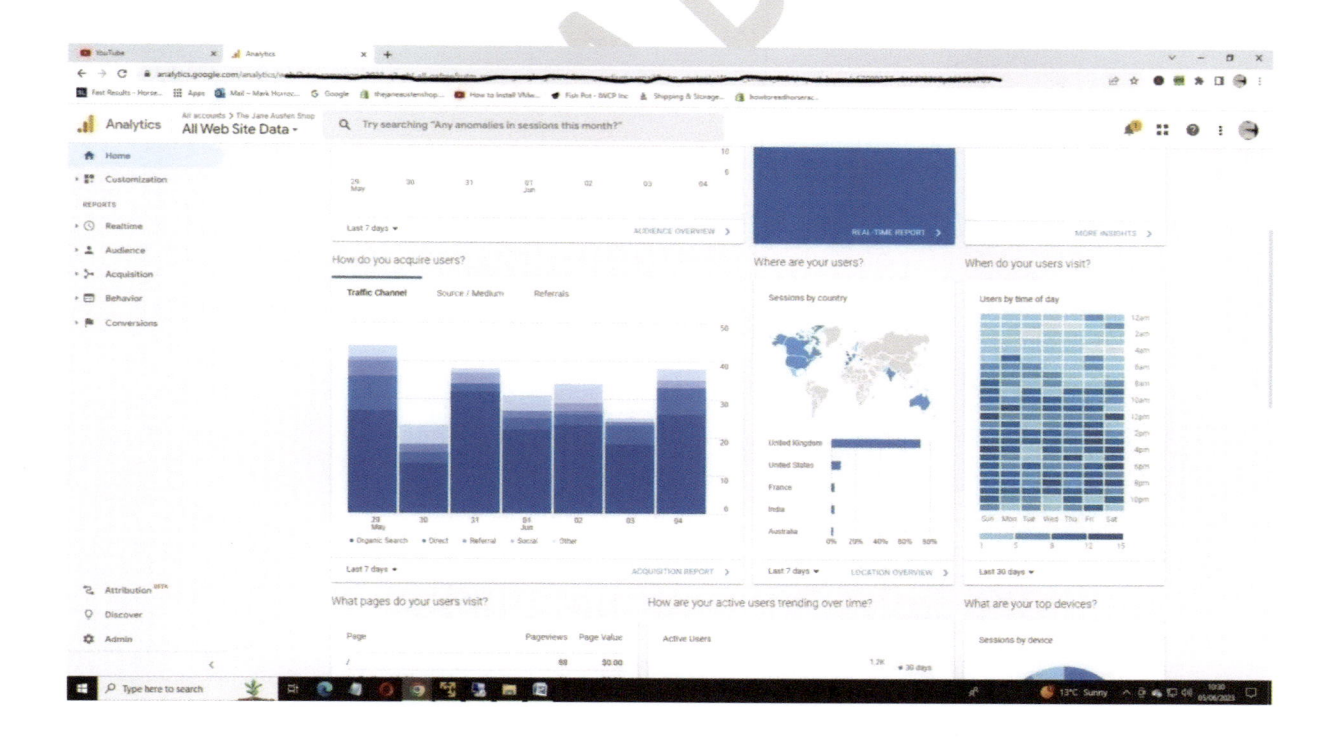

Facebook

https://www.facebook.com/

I tried paid advertising on Facebook and I will be quite candid about this I never really had any success with this social media platform. I found targeting customers was difficult plus I did not like the configuration. I found Google Adwords far superior and it generated most of my sales via this platform. The only benefit I got from Facebook was creating a free Facebook page to promote my products or services for free.

Bing

https://www.bing.com/

This is a paid per click – PPC platform that works similar to Google Adwords but this did not really generate enough website traffic for my websites. I tried Bing for about a year and really did not get much traction. It is very similar to configure like Adwords and I found the cost per click for keywords was similar to Adwords.

Pinterest

https://www.pinterest.co.uk/

I strongly recommend this social media site for promoting your products for free I never used paid product promotions on Pinterest. This free traffic was great and I certainly achieved sales and the best thing it was for free.

Organic Traffic

https://chevanderwheil.com/

This is my second preference to acquire website traffic with Google Adwords PPC being the best method. Organic traffic takes time to acquire and requires dedication and the ability to write natural content in product descriptions or blogs. When a potential customer enters a search term, for example **'rare teddy bear'**, if your website or products are displayed on the first page of the Google search engine then you would certainly get organic traffic. I created a website many years ago that was about UK horse racing betting however this was not eligible for Google Adwords PPC due to the subject content being gambling. This meant I had to write many articles over a period of two years with search terms that I knew potential customers would be using.

If you go to the menu option **Articles** on my website https://chevanderwheil.com/ you can see how many articles I have written. This website now ranks very well on Google see screenshot below.

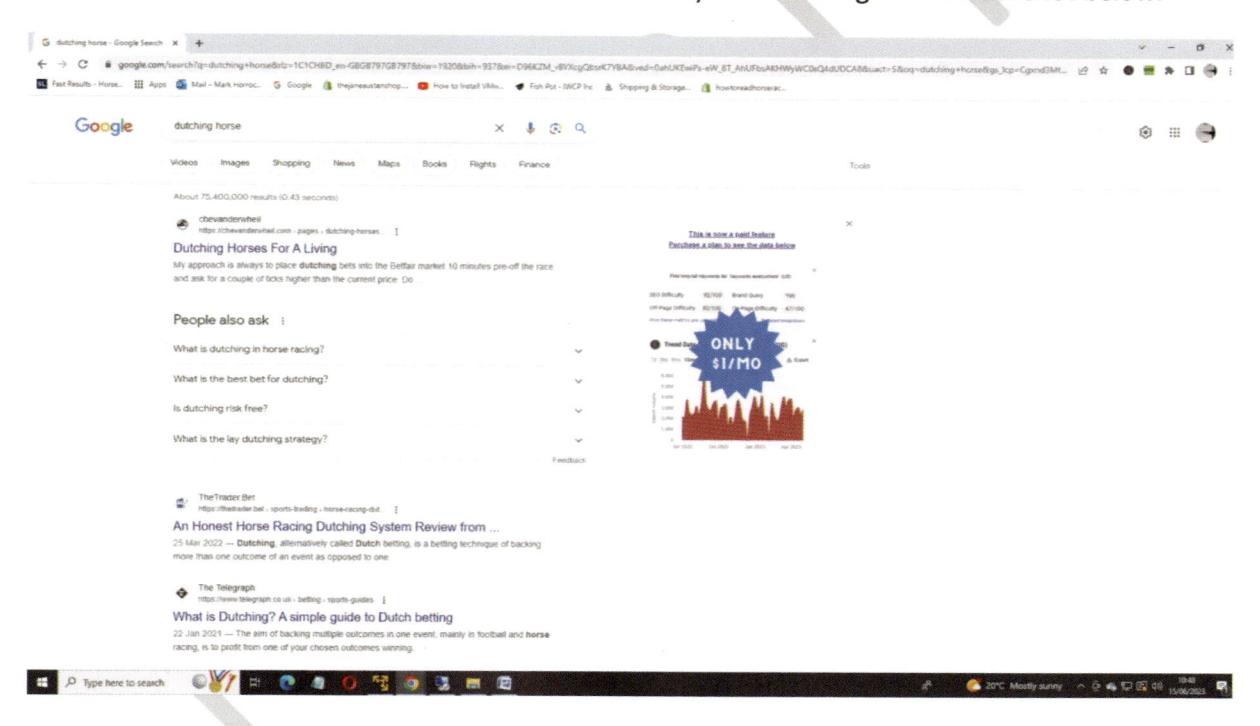

The search term is **dutching horses** and you can see my website is 1st on page 1 of Google out of 75,400,000 results - pretty impressive!

Organic traffic is free and that is what I love but it requires work. Artificial intelligence (AI) is now all the rage such as **ChatGPT** and it is being used to write content for product descriptions and blogs and websites. My view on this is that it does not produce natural content and lacks any emotion. I prefer to write my own content as I enjoy writing.

Overall and having tried all five methods to acquire traffic I found that I had the most success with Google Adwords. This is not surprising because the Google search engine is the most used worldwide. "To google" has become part of everyday language and is actually classified as a verb in the Oxford English Dictionary, and if you do not believe it then try googling it! However with the increased use of artificial intelligence (AI) this position might change in the future so watch this space.

How To Make Money Idea Number 3

Flippa – Selling Digital Assets

https://flippa.com/

This is a great platform to make money by selling digital assets like domain names, websites, Apps and many more. I have implemented many Shopify online retail stores and these businesses were established over a couple of months with profitable sales which I then sold on Flippa. Please see screenshot below of a recent sale of a retail website for US $5000.

I love this way of making money it's very exciting and profitable I thoroughly recommend it.

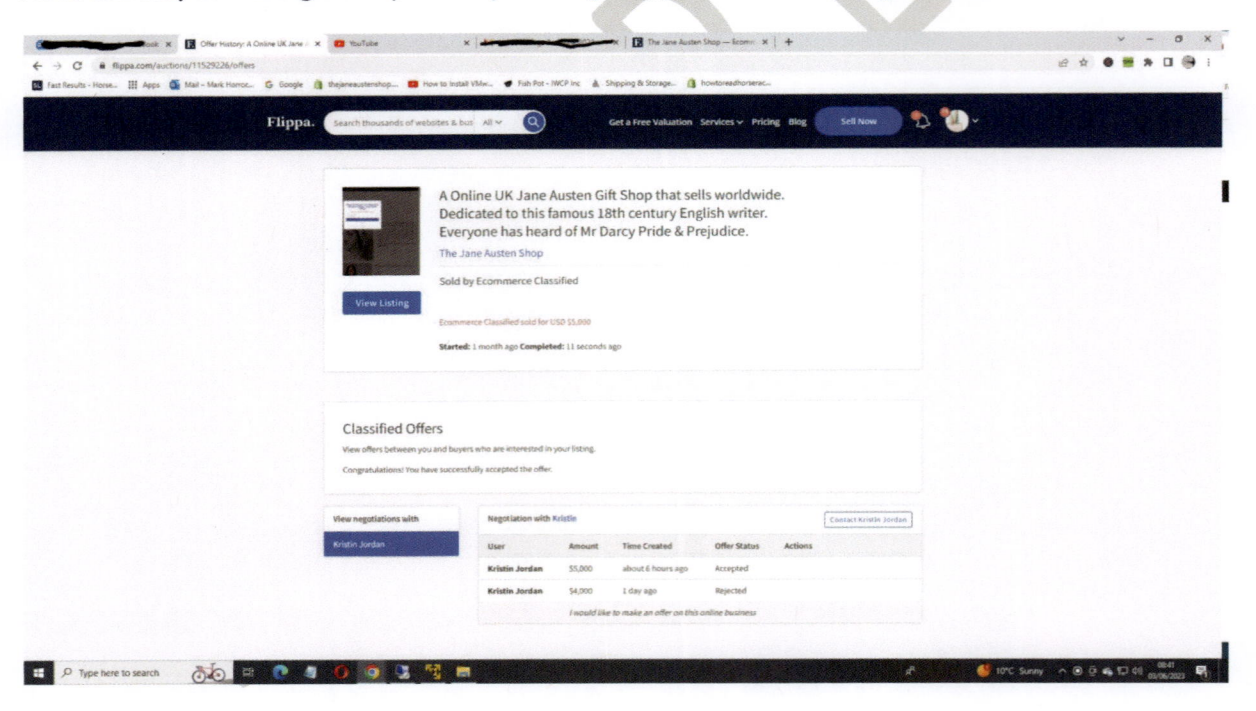

Another website I created I sold in about 6 weeks for US $2900. I actually regretted selling this site as it had proven sales and great potential. It was a drop shipping website selling light up shoes for children and adults.

Using paid traffic via Google Adwords it achieved sales very quickly the cost per click was quite high but the profit margins were great and could accommodate this.

Once you find a niche and a market you can create a Shopify website in days get the business generating sales using Adwords PPC to get traffic and then sell it on Flippa for a nice profit.

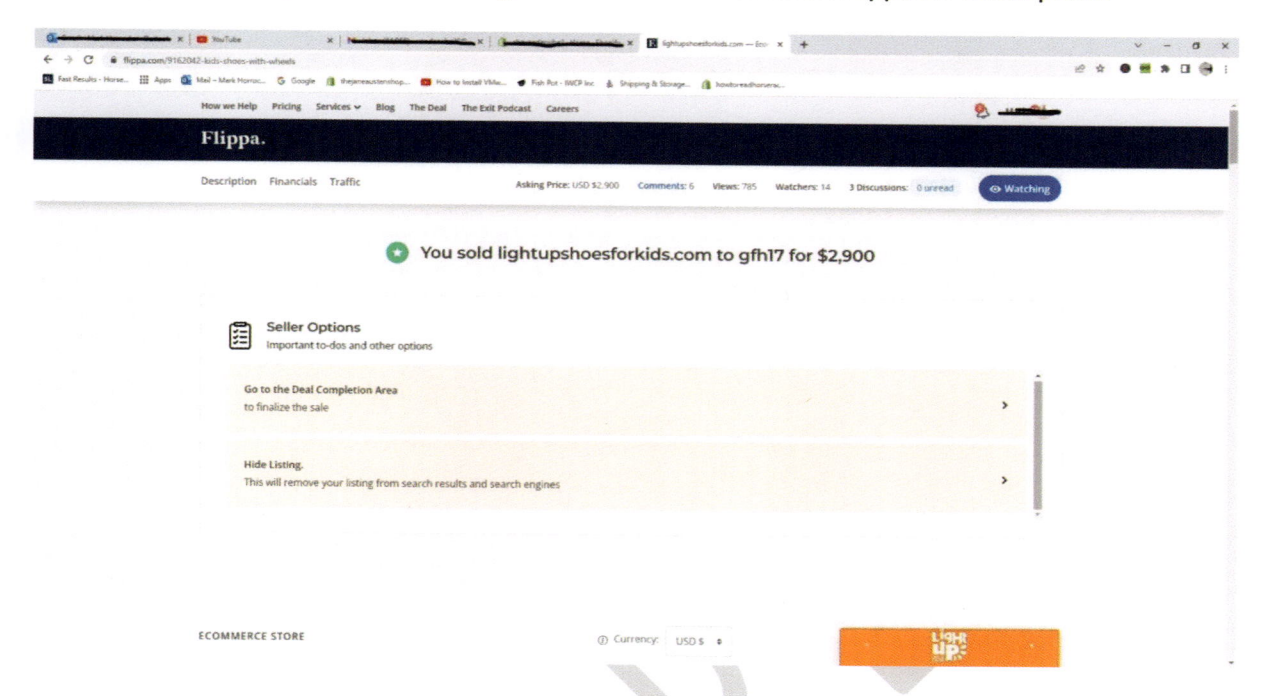

How To Make Money Idea Number 4

Udemy – Sell Your Own Online Courses

https://www.udemy.com/

This is a great platform to create and sell your own online video courses. If you are an expert in your field then creating a course should not take that long. I created a course on reading UK horse racing form which generates a passive income every month 24x7. Now horse racing has always been my passion and I have written many books on this subject. The course took a week from writing the course and for it to go live on the Udemy website.

Please see screenshot below my course is pointed to by the blue line.

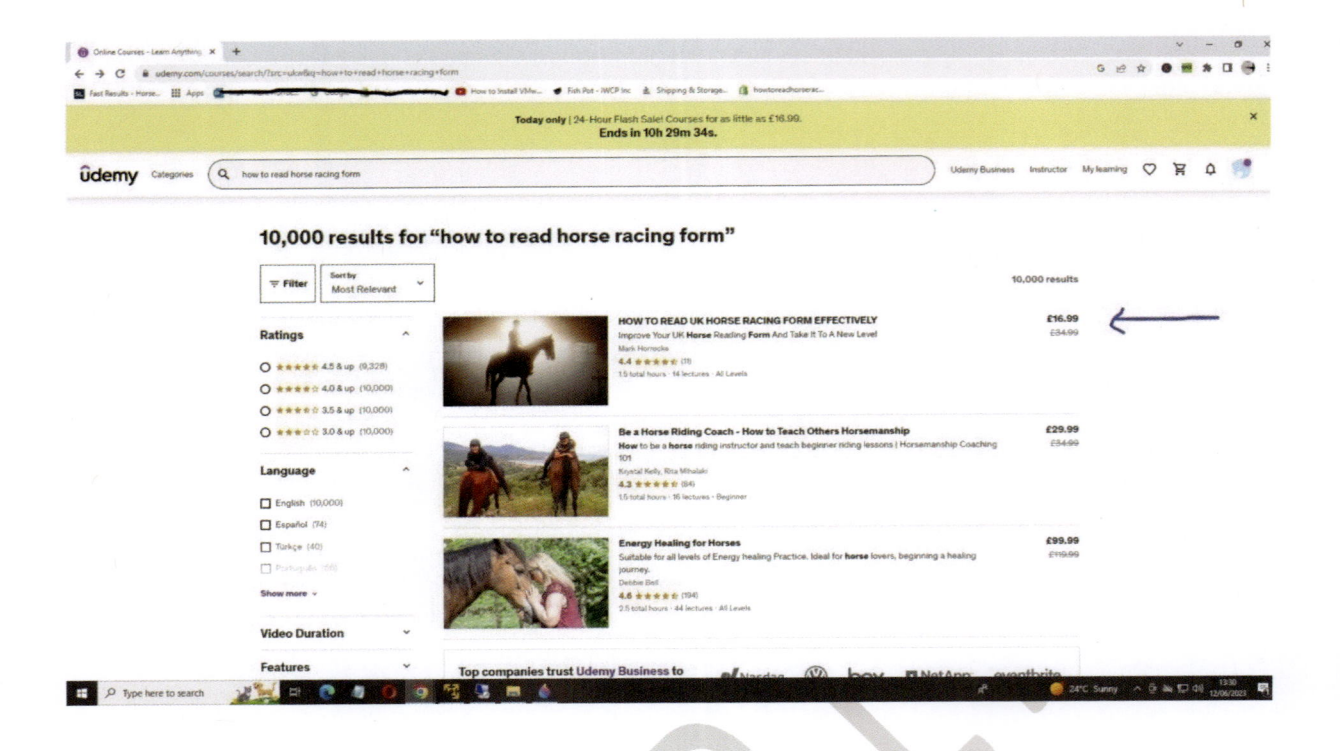

The course sells for £16.99 and I wrote this particular course in 2021 and it has good reviews.

You can register with **Udemy.com** for free as an instructor and then create your online video course. Once you have finished creating your course you upload this to Udemy and then wait for confirmation that is has gone live.

This is a great way to make passive income from your own personal skills. If you can create a number of online video courses then this will enable you to scale your passive income.

I can recommend you create an online video course it is worth it.

How To Make Money Idea Number 5

Amazon Kindle

https://kdp.amazon.com/

I stumbled on to this by accident and was a bit sceptical at first but it is certainly an excellent way to make a passive income. Everyone knows about Amazon you can now write eBooks and paperback books and list these on Amazon kindle for sale. You will get royalties for each book you sell. The amount of royalty is dependent on the price of the book. Amazon handles all of the sales and printing so it is totally hands free.

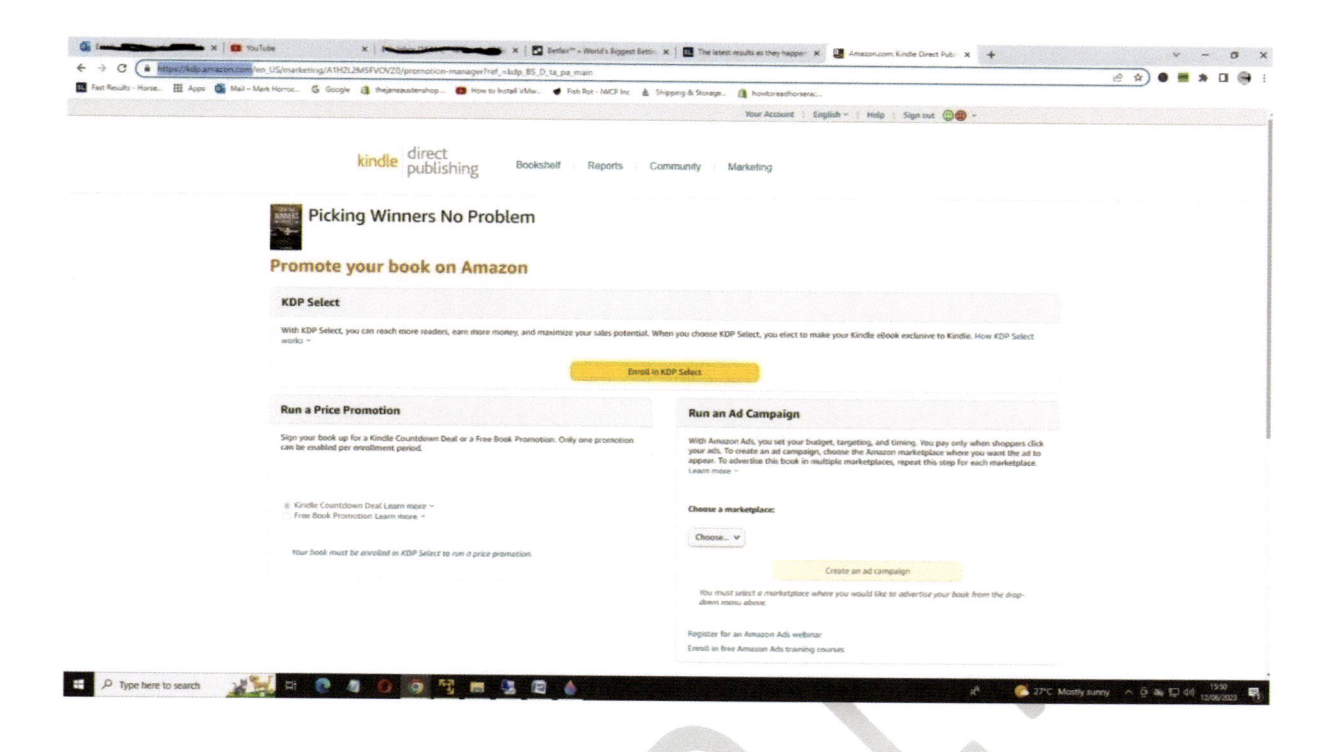

I have written approximately 17 books around the subject of UK horse racing in eBook and paperback formats Kindle have just recently added a hardback book option.

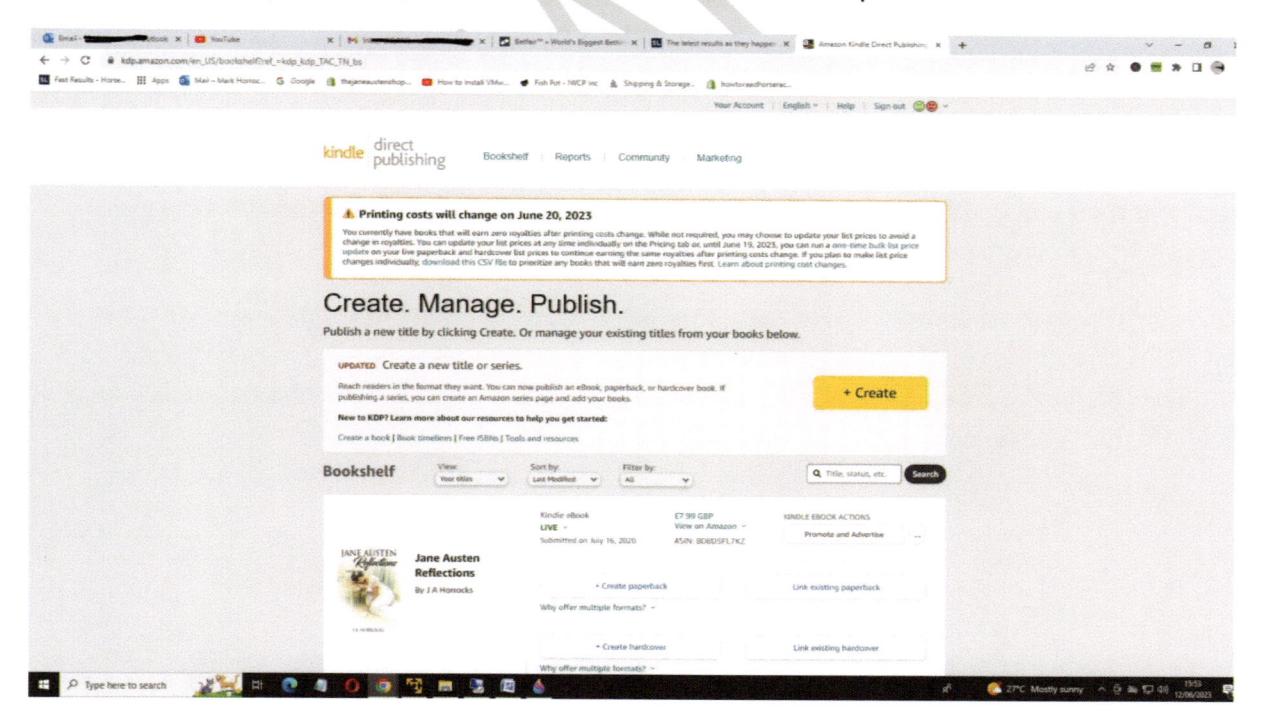

In the screenshot below you can see a couple of my horse racing books and their retail price.

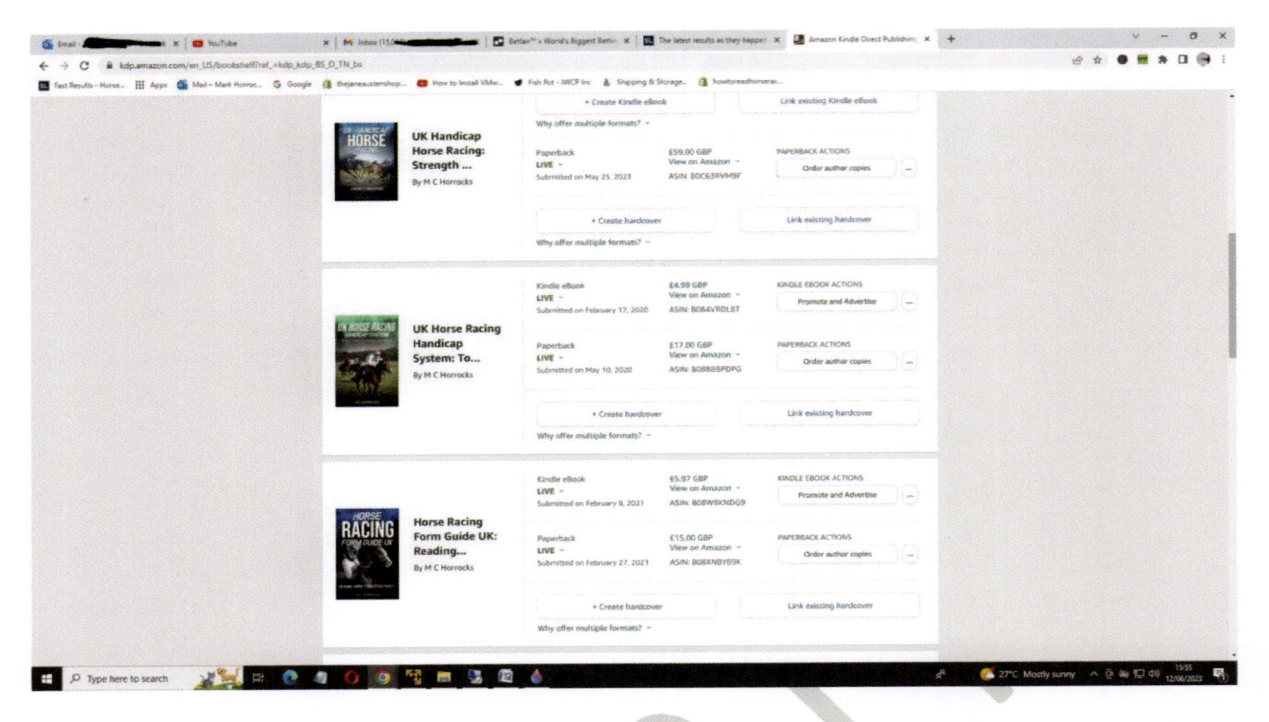

At the end of each month you are paid your royalties which varies depending on how many books you sell. It is important you charge the correct price for your books if they are too cheap you will make little money. I played around with my book prices until I hit a sweet spot. You have a dashboard which displays by country what your royalties are and how many of each book you have sold.

I always remember my first book going live and in the first hour I made money I was quite impressed and I still today check the book sales on a daily basis.

It is important you find the right niche and make sure the market is not saturated. This is a great passive income source and I thoroughly recommend it.

Once I had written a number of books about UK horse racing I decided to create a website using the excellent ecommerce platform Shopify and sell these books on there as well. The main reason I did this was that I could make more money. Some of my books sell for £50 so this would mean a large profit to me. See my website screenshot below.

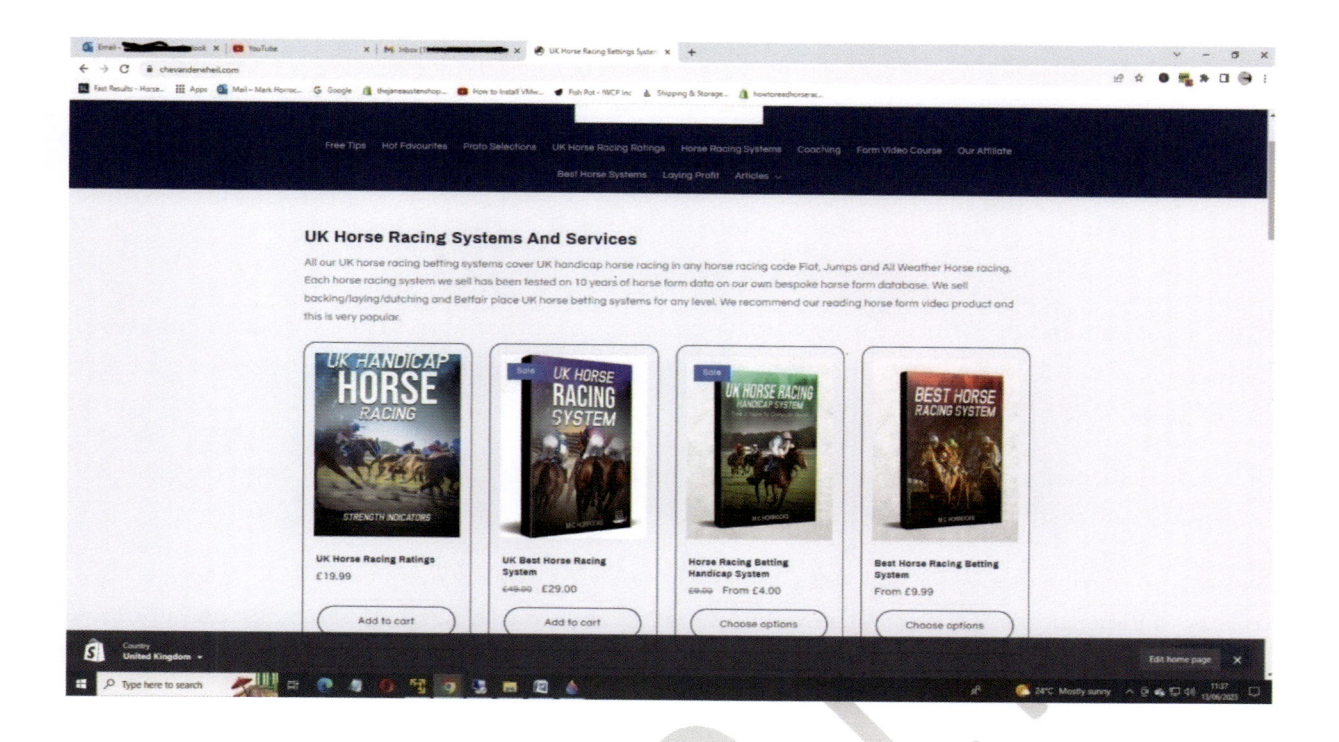

My website is https://chevanderwheil.com/

I have to post the paperback books to the customer so this is not passive but it is worth it due to the large profit return. The eBooks I simply just email to the customer. I want to touch on an important subject and that is your email subscriber list. I offer a free eBook when customers sign up with their email address on my website and this has allowed me to build up a large email database. I use this email list to promote special offers and it pays off as my revenue has certainly increased. There is an old saying the money is in the list!

How To Make Money Idea Number 6

Betfair Trading

https://www.betfair.com/

This is my favourite way of making a passive income and this is certainly not an easy market to enter. Many try and many fail in the pursuit of this income generating method. Now you might think that I have gone mad and the answer is no and I will explain how I make money using Betfair. Now Betfair is a betting/trading exchange that covers most sports but the ones I concentrate on are UK and Irish horse racing. I must stress I am not betting on horses I am actually trading on horses. When you bet on a horse you win money when the horse wins the race and the opposite if it loses the race. When you trade horses you might back a horse at decimal odds 4.0 which is 3/1 in old money and then lay the horse at lower decimal odds 3.0 which is 2/1. This gives us you a profit if the lay side gets matched. If we had £10 at decimal odds 4.0 this would give us a £40 return less the £30 on the lay side which gives us a £10 profit, obviously both the back and lay sides of the trade have to get matched.

Now I have automated this process via a Bot (Software) which runs on a VPS – virtual private server so I can monitor this anywhere in the world. I have actually done this from a smart phone on a beach in Barbados!

This money making idea takes time to implement and you cannot purchase these bots I developed this myself and tested it using real money.

This way of making money will not suit everyone but this is a prime example of a market that is hard to enter and be successful. If you can crack this market you can scale quickly and make some serious money.

I am fortunate as I love horse racing and this way of making money is an extension to this.

How To Make Money Idea Number 7

Sell on eBay

I touched on selling eBay affiliate products in an earlier in this chapter I will describe my journey selling my own products on eBay. These products were purchased from various wholesalers in the UK and Ireland. My main niche was fishing as I was a keen fisherman in my youth and I am still today. So I homed in on fishing lures for all types of fishing but I was keen on one brand of fishing lure and decided to purchase £2000 of these they were £3.25 each at cost price. I could sell these at approximately £7 or this is what I thought! I listed the various lures on eBay and waited for the sales to come in. Now I had 100's of these lures so I was keen to start getting a return on my financial outlay. The days and weeks would pass and the sales were very slow so I started lowering the price. This is when I realised I had not done my due diligence I realised the market was saturated I had not checked my competition. It took me over a year to sell all of the £2000 of lures I kept two of these lures to remind me of my failings.

I only sell used items on eBay now as a little money spinner and this is quite fun. I mentioned earlier I have written books which I sell on my website I also sell these on eBay and these are unique so there is no competition. These horse racing books are good sellers on eBay and this proves the advantage of having your own product. This also allows for larger mark ups and more profit on sales.

My personal opinion is that eBay is saturated and customers are demanding lower prices for everything on this platform.

Conclusions

I hope this has given you an insight into my journey with 7 making money ideas and what you have to be aware of if you start this journey. I will highlight the key points from this book.

Road To Entry

This is very important if the market is saturated then do not try to compete as there is too much competition. You will most likely end up in a price war and make little profit. If everyone for example is selling dog collars sourced from Aliexpress and you are trying to sell on eBay then you will struggle. You will get sales but it will not scale I tried many products from Aliexpress only to find 100s of other people selling these products.

Ensure You Have Control

This is a key point you need to have control of your making money ideas and I like selling my own products and services. I mentioned in the book how I write my own books and Betfair trading bots so I have control of these making money ideas. Plus I have no competition and the profits are large with no price wars. I strongly recommend creating your own products and services and turn them into making money ideas. I would say this is one of the most important things I have learnt through my journey.

Prepare To Lose Money

I spent a large amount trying new making money ideas especially around Google Adwords PPC – Pay Per Click this was due to lack of experience. Holding onto stock purchases for over a year due to poor sales and then having to basically reduce the retail price as close to the wholesale price I paid for these products was also costly. Yes you can start making money ideas for free as I mentioned in this book but it is a long game and you need money now.

SEO And Organic Traffic

This was a game changer for me once I understand the power of natural content and ranking on page one on the Google search engine then I started to get website traffic for free. There are no short cuts here and ignore stupid emails from people who state they will get you on page one of Google. Understand your customer search terms and convey this in your content and also try to add value.

The Money Is In The List

Building an email subscriber list from your website or blog is crucial I make more money via weekly promotions sometimes daily. I also include automatic follow up emails when potential customers have browsed my products or services. This works, I always get a smile when I see an email marketing campaign executed and watch the sales come in. Offer a freebie on your email popup window to attract more email subscribers to your website or blog.

I hope you have enjoyed this book take harder decisions now for an easier life later!

Printed in Great Britain
by Amazon